Working Together

Recommendations from the findings of the

AWSNA Pedagogical Advisors' Colloquium

July 2006

Printed with support from the
Waldorf Educational Foundation and from another
Foundation wishing to remain anonymous

Published by:

Waldorf Publications at the

Research Institute for Waldorf Education

38 Main Street

Chatham, NY 12037

Title: *Working Together: An Introduction to Pedagogical
Mentoring in Waldorf Schools*
Authors: PAC participants with Virginia Flynn, Ann Matthews,
Else Göttgens
Editor: David Mitchell
Proofreader: Ann Erwin
© 2006 by AWSNA
Reprinted 2014 Waldorf Publications
ISBN # 978-1-936367-64-1

Table of Contents

Foreword

Rudolf Steiner had a strong vision for the future of humanity. His every indication was for us as students of anthroposophy to continually strive to create cultural institutions where true individual freedom and diversity can live. Waldorf schools are a testimony to Steiner's picture of an ever-alive and developing cultural community. Waldorf schools do not have the usual checks and balances found in educational institutions where school principals, headmasters/mistresses or department heads oversee the quality of the teaching. Instead, each Waldorf teacher strives individually in the classroom and works with colleagues in a learning, educational community. This is done in accordance with his or her conscience and will. We Waldorf teachers are grateful to be able to work in freedom, a freedom where our own initiative and capacities allow us to be humanly creative.

What does this mean? Beginning with a thorough study of the Waldorf curriculum and then embracing the principal of "working out of anthroposophy," a path of self development, the Waldorf teacher realizes one can never fully reach the ultimate or top level in one's work. There is always more to learn. Each child, class or even decade changes previously known 'ways' of teaching. The Waldorf teacher continually strives to "read the moment" and create a lively class atmosphere for the students, where they feel known and challenged. Inherent in Waldorf teaching is working with the unfolding child in a conscious, open mode allowing the rigors and excellence of the class curriculum to develop capacities. With the help of working with the anthroposophical picture of the unfolding human being, Waldorf teachers try consciously to teach not for immediate results, but for the future, where lasting capacities and skills will serve the student for life.

Rudolf Steiner described teaching as an art. Waldorf schools respect and encourage differences in "styles" of each teacher. But, as with all fine artists, basic skills must be mastered and understandings become "second nature" before interpretation and inspiration take hold.

This sounds good in the ideal, but given the Waldorf school community without a hierarchical structure, where individual "freedom" in the classroom reigns, many questions arise.

- How can we be assured in our school that the quality of the teaching and the depth of understanding of Waldorf education grow stronger each year?
- How do we know what our colleagues are doing in the classroom?
- What is the best way to support a new teacher?
- Where can we go with our questions and inevitable struggles as teachers?
- Are there agreements we can reach as an Association on best principles of mentoring and basic benchmarks for each grade?

It was out of this thinking that the regional leaders of the Association of Waldorf Schools of North America back in 2002 recognized the need to bring together, from all over the continent, experienced teachers who mentor for collaboration on professionalism in teaching in Waldorf schools. There were then, and are now, schools with excellent mentoring and evaluation programs. There were and are schools that are struggling to exist. The Pedagogical Advisors' Colloquium was founded to raise the awareness for the need for networking in strengthening mentoring and evaluation in all schools. In keeping with Steiner's indications, mentoring, like teaching, is an art requiring certain basic understandings for a foundation.

It is our hope that the regional seminars and workshops on mentoring and evaluation that have grown out of the Pedagogical Advisors' Colloquium will provide new enthusiasm for supporting and expanding programs in every school. Such programs assure parents and colleagues that a level of professionalism lives in the school.

We hope this booklet, written from our findings, will serve mentors and school faculties in "raising the bar" and deepening the support for Waldorf teaching.

– Virginia Flynn

Group at PAC Seminar in Glouchester, MA

Eurythmy with Leonore Russell

Introduction

This booklet, ***Working Together,*** is one of the outcomes of the AWSNA Pedagogical Advisors' Colloquium, a group that began working in the spring of 2002. Formed initially to support AWSNA in the development of pedagogical advisory services, this group of teachers was mandated by the AWSNA Delegates and invited as experienced colleagues from various parts of North America to work in collaboration towards the furthering of excellence in Waldorf education. Our movement has many groups and individuals working towards this end. The specific task of this group is described in the following pages.

The initial focus was to concern ourselves with the successes and challenges facing our movement, particularly in relation to the education of children in classes 1 through 8. Meeting twice yearly, the Pedagogical Advisors' Colloquium (PAC) took up pedagogical research in relation to the development of the child and how the curriculum best serves this development. Some of the topics were: an in-depth study of the nature of the etheric; the development of capacities for observation; educational support work and helping the child overcome hindrances; practical aspects of mentoring a colleague; inner development and social work in relation to the adult; essential aspects of Waldorf education; developing capacities and skills in the students; and didactic considerations of effective teaching practices.

We especially appreciate the many colleagues who joined us as presenters including Else Göttgens, Dennis Klocek, Philip Incao, MD, Cynthia Hoven, Leonore Russell, Ingun Schneider, Jaimen McMillan, Ernst Schuberth, PhD, Mary Jo Oresti, Joan Ingalls and Anniken Mitchell, MA, LPC.

The PAC members have taken initiative in their regional areas by calling together groups of teachers who are already engaged in the work of mentoring and who seek further collaboration in order to increase their effectiveness. Out of these mentor collaboration seminars, the collective experiences of these colleagues have informed our efforts. We are most grateful to the teachers who have already joined in this vital work by attending the seminars and sharing their perspectives. One of the contributions of the mentor collaboration seminars in the west was the development of the document ***"Criteria for Healthy Waldorf Classrooms,* "** which has been adopted by the PAC group and is included in the Appendix of this booklet.

As the PAC members continued their work, it became clear that we could attempt to articulate a few of the "best practices" in areas where we were all in agreement. Other areas can be viewed as opportunities for continued research and exploration. This booklet is something that we hope you will find useful and inspiring. It is offered as an introduction to schools and mentors to support the development of an area which is now realized as an essential ingredient for our success as a movement: ***the art of mentoring.***

– Ann Matthews

AWSNA Pedagogical Advisors' Colloquium: Kathy Brunetta, Jacqueline Develle, Nettie Fabrie, Virginia Fish, Virginia Flynn, Susan Goldstein, Else Göttgens, Gerry LoDolce, Monica Lander, Ann Matthews, Virginia McWilliams, James Pewtherer, Ron Richardson, Leonore Russell and Stephen Sheen

Other participants: David Blair, Torin Finser, PhD, Francina Graef, Flora Jane Hartford, Scott Olmsted and Kathryn Humphrey

Aspects of the booklet which are specific contributions of particular PAC members are credited by the initials of the individual.

Here we can see the new mysteries in action. Two people (or more) initiate each other in a certain area of spiritual experience. The spiritual perception of one person sounds forth in the soul of the other and leads to new insights.

– Dennis Klocek

Considerations for Schools

**An Example of Mentoring Practice
in the Elementary Grades**

He was struggling with his teaching. The hours of preparation were not translating into a healthy class experience. He needed help. When you approached his classroom, it sounded like a disturbed wasps' nest. When you knocked, he opened the door with a face flushed with embarrassment. The children were running everywhere. One child was on the floor screaming. The teacher's attempts to restore order were short-lived.

Three weeks later, when you approached his classroom, it sounded like a contented beehive. When you knocked, he opened the door with a friendly smile. The children looked up and quickly went back to their work. One little girl whispered to her neighbor as she shared her work.

What had happened? He had worked with a mentor who helped him develop his own connection to his class. This gave the children the teaching for which they really had been waiting. (EG)

**Working Together Towards Excellence
in Waldorf Education**

Any time a teacher shows interest in the work of a colleague, a mentoring moment exists. Mentoring is about learning, about support, about interest and about professional development.

How often do we lose teachers because they did not receive the help they needed? How many students do we lose because they are disappointed? How many experienced teachers, with gifts to share, are as yet unaware they are needed? How many have not been supported by their schools to work as mentors? How many teachers find that they are enriched and re-enlivened in their own teaching by assisting a colleague to find new approaches and perspectives?

One School's Experience with Mentoring

During the 1993–1994 school year, the Seattle Waldorf School hired a "school mentor" to work with teachers of classes 1 through 8. They invited an experienced teacher with a wide Waldorf teaching background to come to the school for one year. She was there every day of the week and worked with all of the teachers, including the specialty teachers. Class teachers were visited for three consecutive days during main lessons on a rotating basis. Every teacher had two mentoring hours scheduled with the mentor during the week.

Together they worked on classroom management and understanding the curriculum in the light of the development of the child. There was time for planning blocks and weekly schedules. Attention was given to the students' work and to the quality of their main lesson books. Special attention was given to particular students. Topics were taken up in the faculty meetings with a concentrated approach.

It was an inspiring year for the school and for the visiting mentor. One result was that the upper grades students became more confident in their learning process. The quality of teaching improved overall. Most important for the school, the enrollment began to increase substantially after this year. The mentor kept in contact with the school during the following years and made several shorter visits. This case provides a wonderful example of the importance of mentoring in the success of the teachers. (NF)

When mentoring becomes an integral part of every school's practices, we will see collegial working deepen, where teachers share with one another the gifts they have. We can take responsibility to help one another become better teachers. Nothing less than excellence in Waldorf education is appropriate, and we must dedicate ourselves to work together to make it happen.

Establishing a good mentoring program is part of a healthy Waldorf school community. It supports ongoing inquiry and a lifelong culture of learning, and it demonstrates responsibility and care for its teachers. These are necessary prerequisites for mentoring.

Effective Mentoring

An effective mentoring program should be designed to suit the school's needs matched with whatever experience and capacity the school can offer. What does your school need? What resources does your school have? What can you offer? How does the school create a culture that values this work? How does a new teacher meet the culture of a school? **For** the **beginning teacher** – how does he or she meet the children? Does the teaching relate to the curriculum? How does he or she meet the parents, plan the year, etc.?

- For the **experienced teacher** needing sustaining support – how does he or she continue to enliven the lessons?

- For the **teacher in crisis** – how does he or she rebuild inner strength and insight? How does one sustain sound practices to meet the challenges?

- **All teachers,** whether they are class teachers, specialists, high school teachers or early childhood educators, benefit from mentoring.

- Mentoring does not substitute for a certified Waldorf teacher education program. If necessary, schools will bear the responsibility to see that adequate training is obtained by their teachers, starting right from the time of the hiring decision.

Examples of Mentoring Styles or Approaches

- **In-house mentors** are our colleagues. They are chosen for their people skills or by peer mentors because of their experience and success in the classroom.

- **External mentors** will bring new perspectives and insights and devote concentrated, focused time for teachers with immediate and extended assistance.

- In **small group work,** teachers can gather in departmental meetings for subject-focused work, curriculum development and study time for teachers of a specific class or age group. Inexperienced teachers can receive informal advice during these gatherings. Experienced teachers can learn from each other.

- In **faculty development activities,** we can encourage and support colleagues to do their research and then share their work. Some examples of this type of activity: A colleague might research what Rudolf Steiner actually advised about certain aspects of the curriculum, as it is practiced now, such as in the classes of astronomy or meteorology. Another colleague may compile a manual for how reading is taught in the lower grades, etc.

- **Faculty meetings** may increasingly take on aspects of a "learning academy" where teachers share their pedagogical work, support one another in the nurturing of new skills and become more actively involved in the education of all students and the development of the curriculum.

- **Team evaluation** involves several mentors visiting the school together. This is a dynamic and effective way for a school to receive immediate feedback from a number of perspectives about programs, school culture and overall teaching.

Implementing In-House Mentoring

A great aid, and one which requires little financial investment, is the "flip-flop" main lesson schedule. One day a week, a coordinating mentor's class, usually an upper grade, has a specialty subject or two taught during main lesson time and then has main lesson after the morning recess. This enables the coordinating mentor or a colleague, on a weekly basis, to visit other classes or to substitute during the morning main lesson period so that another colleague can visit in a mentoring role.

The Difference between Mentoring and Evaluation

Like mentoring, evaluation involves having interest in a teacher's practice and in educational excellence. Unlike mentoring, an evaluator's relationship is not only with the teacher, but also with the school, the group, or the individual in the school holding responsibility for professional growth and development. The evaluation process is also intended to support and encourage a teacher's growth and to ensure that the quality of teaching reflects the principles and ideals of Waldorf education.

As an advocate, ultimately for the children, an evaluator's responsibility is to describe what is taking place in the classroom, to discern what the teacher is doing well and to discover areas where the teacher may require further skill development to meet the childrens' needs. Through a process of observation and conversation, the evaluator may make recommendations that mentoring is needed. The evaluator is not the person who will provide the mentoring. It is essential also that the evaluator is not the same individual who is the teacher's mentor. The mentor is working in a confidential relationship and does not provide an evaluative report to the school.

The report written by an evaluator documents the evaluation process and includes a summary of observations and conversation, with commendations and recommendations for the teacher that the school and teacher put into practice. This report is a confidential document intended for the teacher and the appropriate school committee only.

An evaluation may in some cases be part of a school's process where, for example, a teacher is graduated from a probationary contract. However, evaluation does not replace a faculty or school's responsibility for implementing and sustaining effective employment practices. An evaluator does not determine ongoing employment or termination.

An evaluation can assist with a teacher's self-reflective practices and help make clear where ongoing development is needed. A teacher benefits most from an evaluation when he or she welcomes and invites the process and contributes to the evaluator's efforts with focused self-reflective practice.

Considerations for the Individual Mentor

The Mentor

Here are two polar-opposite comments from two – currently very successful – teachers:

a. "I was on the verge of quitting after the visits of that 'mentor!' I felt ready for the garbage bin."
b. "I was all set to quit when that mentor came to see me and showed me how to turn my capacities to their best use."

From the first (a) teacher: "I was a terrible teacher. I realize now just how poorly I was doing. My (in-house) mentor had already had several sessions with me and had told me in no uncertain terms all that was expected from a Waldorf teacher. There were many areas to be developed – having to know all the material by heart, not using any notes or books during presentations, never raising my voice indoors, imposing total silence during work time, etc., etc., etc.

"And then a new mentor came to the classroom. Yes, it was not very tidy, but you should have seen her nose wrinkle in disdain! And in the conversation after her visit – oh, boy! There was 'no proper image used for the multiplication of fractions, the book work was not tidy enough,' and on and on she went. It took me more than a year to get back my enjoyment in teaching. I can see now, of course, that she was right in everything she said, but was it helpful? No – rather the opposite."

And from the second (b) teacher: "We had already had a few talks, during which she listened to my fears and concerns. When she came to my class, she looked at the children's animals in clay. She said that she could never get her own students to do animals so characteristically and that I must have described them very well!

"There was no word about the messy classroom or my untidy desk during our first visit. When we spoke the morning verse, I could feel 'the loving light of the Sun' in her warm, meaningful participation.

"After I had told the children some facts about water animals, she raised her hand and asked if she might contribute a story from her childhood. She then told a story about her father's crocodile hunting days that had the whole class in stitches.

"In our conversation after the lesson, she first asked the kind of questions that made me realize where my strengths were. She then asked the same kind of questions which made me aware of some of the areas I could develop in myself and in my teaching. I doubt that I could have continued as a teacher without her help."

(EG)

Why Become a Mentor?

A mentoring relationship is just that – a relationship. It is not a monologue, but a dialogue. Thus, the mentor has the opportunity in the mentoring relationship to learn, grow and deepen his or her own understanding of Waldorf education.

A beginning relationship with an inexperienced teacher will include elements of forthright instruction by the mentor that are different from the interaction between two experienced colleagues. However, it is the sign of a healthy mentoring relationship when both colleagues become re-inspired through the mentoring process.

Basic Criteria for Mentoring

1. A good mentor has a willingness to assist and to support another teacher and to strive with them to realize the essence of Waldorf pedagogy. On this path, one learns to discern the possibilities in another rather than to criticize imperfections.

2. A mentor is a person who feels rooted in – and is actively working out of – anthroposophy. A mentor can articulate the essence of the Waldorf curriculum and child development out of his own life experience.

3. A mentor who has been a successful Waldorf teacher is more credible than one who has not. Having taught the grade the mentee is teaching is equally most desirable.

4. Inner strength springing from conviction will enable a mentor to be straightforward and candid, when necessary.

5. A mentor has tact, respect and accountability.

6. A mentor is someone who can work in a confidential relationship.

Taking the First Steps Towards Establishing the Mentor/Mentee Relationship

Pedagogical mentoring is viewed as a professional opportunity leading to growth and development for both the mentor and the mentee. Here are a few recommended essentials that many experienced mentors have found helpful to minimize the stress of a working mentoring relationship and make it as comfortable as possible. Take time to develop a rapport by exchanging experiences. The relationship begins with taking interest in the other person.

- Explore general areas: family, health, worries, ambitions...
- Share how you discovered Waldorf education.
- Converse about essential aspects of the education.
- Share your teaching backgrounds and significant experiences.
- Speak about your mentoring experiences and expectations of mentoring.

Then move the conversation to cover more specific professional issues:

- How do you prepare for your lessons?
- How do you track student progress?
- How do you record observations on students?

Review the confidential aspect of the mentor/mentee relationship and the significance of this in context of the various school bodies. If the mentor takes notes during the visit, speak together about what will be done with the notes. Conclude by expressing appreciation to the mentee for allowing this visit in his or her classroom.

Preparing for a Visit: Before Entering the Classroom
1. Arrange a preliminary conversation or exchange in which the following areas are addressed:
   a. Ask the teacher to provide a seating chart for the classroom. This will give the mentor a better opportunity to observe specific children for reflection together afterwards.
   b. Review the schedule for your classroom observations – main lesson, recess and other lessons.
   c. Agree on an appropriate time and location of the follow up meeting (s) or conversation (s) so that they are conveniently scheduled in a timely fashion with ample time allotted. A minimum of one and one half hour on the same day is recommended.

d. Request that the teacher collect samples of the students' work. An effective collection might be work from groups of 3 or 4 students each whose work is above average, average and below average, to indicate skill levels in math, composition and main lesson books. There might also be a sample of the students' practice books.

2. It is important to remember that you are there to observe the teacher and the children working together. While certain individual children will attract your attention, you should strive to maintain your focus on the whole class and the teacher's interactions with the students. This focus may be shifted on subsequent visits.

3. It is recommended that you arrive early for the classroom visit so that last-minute arrangements can be made, or in case you have not had a chance to review or address the above aspects.

The Visit: Entering the Classroom

Immediately upon entering a classroom, one may see a number of different things from one's own classroom. Be prepared to enjoy the way this teacher manages his or her own classroom.

And now the children start to come in. Be observant. How do they enter? Do they look happy to see their teacher? Do they meet with their eyes? Are they dying to tell something important that happened? Or do quite a few of them try to sneak past the teacher without having to greet him or her? Do several avoid eye contact or are distant during the morning handshake?

The mentor notices and notes down (or remembers), but holds back judgment, as later impressions may contradict these initial observations. Mentoring is a practice involving discernment not judgment. For example, you may initially think a teacher is doing something "completely wrong," only to discover that this is precisely what this group of children needs. (EG)

Most people blossom when given honest acknowledgment of their gifts and capacities. Truly engaging in this practice takes the mentor a long way in maintaining an effective relationship with a colleague. It provides a foundation for humility, discernment and empathy.

The Visit: In the Classroom

To focus the observations it is recommended that the mentors use the list of criteria adopted by the Pedagogical Advisors' Colloquium as a guideline for effective observation and mentoring (see Appendix A: ***Criteria for Healthy Waldorf Classrooms***). In the course of a series of mentoring visits, this list could serve as an aid to the teacher, helping towards self-evaluation. This document may be used in the following ways:

- As a resource to help make healthy observations, free of judgments. It provides a broad spectrum of focus areas: Relationships, Wholeness of the Lesson, Professionalism and Classroom Environment.
- As an aid in preparing for a visit

- As an aid to the teacher
- As an aid in preparing for a written evaluation by some one other than the mentor

To track observations it is both acceptable and important for the mentor to write down the observations during the visits. These notes describe the phenomena of the classroom: time, transitions, activities, behaviors, assignments, etc. Mentors might work from a consistent format and maintain these records as a reference for long-term mentoring. The notes become a confidential record for the teacher and for the mentor to refer to before the next visit or conversation. They are a basis for follow-up conversations and can support the mentor's efforts to be objective.

Two Essential Questions for the Mentor

1. What can this teacher do better than I was able to do as a teacher myself?
2. What am I learning from this relationship?

Interventions and Demonstrations: When and How Situations

You are seated in the back of a Third Grade classroom. The teacher is reading a story and you observe a child crawling under the desk to deliver a note to a classmate. She returns to her seat unnoticed by the teacher. What do you do?

Simply record your observations in your notes. Events in the classroom are points for conversation and not for intervention. To learn how to withhold judgment is an art to be developed by the mentor.

Sometimes the teacher might request, or the mentor might offer, that the mentor demonstrate certain teaching techniques. This should be discussed before the classroom visit and may take the form of a spontaneous contribution or a formal "demonstration."

The Post-Observation Conversation

Out of the life of dreams we awaken each day through the impact of the outer world, through its light and tones and warmth. Out of the isolation of our dreams, we awaken to a certain point into the community of our fellow human beings. We awaken in response to all the various impressions that the sense world makes on us.

Just as a person wakes up sensing light and tone through the natural world surrounding him in everyday life, so do we wake up at a higher level in the encounter with the soul-spirit of our fellow human beings. We begin to develop an understanding for the spiritual world only when we consciously strive to work on the encounter with the soul-spiritual element of our fellow human beings.

> *Human beings wake up in the mutual encounter*
> *with other human beings. As each one has new*
> *experiences between his encounters with these others,*
> *and has grown a little, these awakenings take place*
> *in an ever new way as people go on meeting. The*
> *awakenings undergo a burgeoning [sprouting,*
> *springing] development.*
>
>   – Rudolf Steiner
>   from *Awakening to Community*

Why the Socratic Method?

Here are examples of two kinds of conversations.

Conversation 1:
> Mentor: The children were very restless today. Are you too tired?
>
> Mentee: No, not at all.
>
> > [Gate closed, drawbridge up!]

Conversation 2:
> Mentor: How did you find the children today?
>
> Mentee: Restless. . . .
>
> Mentor: Any idea what the cause might be?
>
> Mentee: Well. I *am* very tired, and perhaps I could not "hold" them enough...
>
> Mentor: Why are you tired?
>
> Mentee: Actually, I stay up late to do my class preparation.
>
> Mentor: Shall we discuss how you prepare? Perhaps I could give you some hints about how to structure your preparation. This would save time, and then you could get more sleep.
>
> > [Gate opens! Welcome sign up!]
>
> > (EG)

The Socratic method is about asking questions rather than providing answers and solutions. The challenge is: How do we find the right questions that will lead to answers and solutions?

To increase a mentor's effectiveness, the mentor will need an opportunity for some soul-searching (inner activity) between the time of the classroom visit and the post-visit conversation. By doing this the mentor can, in effect, give the classroom observations, as well as the personality of the teacher, a chance to "resound inwardly." From this place will come the right questions. Often, something subtle in the behavior of the children will reveal to the mentor what needs to be asked of the teacher. The mentor looks for what this might be.

Mentors often begin with basic questions, such as, "What do you think went well in your lesson today?" and "Is there something you could have done better or differently?" The next questions should then lead toward those areas in need of attention. It is important to remember that part of the task of a mentor is to make it possible for the mentee to become conscious of his or her weaknesses. Those weaknesses may simply be in the realm of "learning how to teach" or may be closely connected with the personality of the teacher. In the first case, dealing with **_didactic_** problems, the teacher may simply need additional basic teaching skills, which the mentor should be able to impart. Experience and tact are indispensable to address concerns in the second category – issues arising from **_personality._** Note that behavior challenges in the classroom can stem from both ineffective teaching and personality-bound issues. A developing teacher will usually genuinely seek input and assistance, but discovering one's weaknesses can be frightening and painful. It must happen in such a way that the teacher will grow and blossom rather than lose confidence.

To make progress while avoiding the quicksand of this anxiety-filled phase of mentoring, questions beyond the basic ones should be formulated in light of the mentee's personality as well as from the insights that emerged during the mentor's "quiet time" mentioned above. In many ways, the mentor, in all humility, must act as a *mirror* for the mentee.

Developing a rapport between mentor and mentee will depend a great deal on the willingness on the part of both individuals to make this relationship a fruitful one. Teaching is about becoming. A key component of change is being able to observe oneself. The mentor can engage in a process of assisting in this "mirroring" of the activities of the teacher with the children so that the teacher has an enhanced opportunity for this self-reflection. Requests for feedback and suggestions that come out of a self-discovery of the need for change can be enlivening for both colleagues.

Through an open rapport in conversation, the mentee arrives at an essential point or a focus on which to ponder and work. The mentor can ask if there is anything the teacher feels that he or she would like to work on or to "try out" from the conversation. It is helpful to listen carefully to what the teacher selects and to choose only one specific aspect of teaching to focus on at a time. This can be reviewed at the next meeting. At the end of each meeting, take a moment to review how it is going for both mentee and mentor.

Rudolf Steiner often gave warm and encouraging recognition to the teachers for the continuous striving needed for this vocation. Our collegial working together through strong mentoring programs, and periodic evaluations will have us all acknowledge our continual striving toward excellence in our service to the students. This is a social as well as individual endeavor for the mentor, teacher, school and wider movement.

For Further Information

If you or your school would like further information about Mentor Collaboration Seminars in your area, please contact Virginia Flynn at vflynn@swbell.net, or the AWSNA office at msoule@awsna.org for Michael Soule, the Leader of Programs and Activities.

> *Rudolf Steiner's very first sentence in the Foundation*
> *Course of the first Waldorf school clearly shows*
> *that he was not interested in just another stream of*
> *pedagogical reform, but rather, he was interested*
> *in spiritual competence. He inaugurated the art of*
> *education for the next several hundred years, saying,*
> *"Our task is not one of intellectual-comfortable*
> *work, but in the highest sense one of moral-spiritual*
> *values." From the very beginning he also mentions*
> *the mandate that we have received from higher*
> *powers.*
>
> *– Heinz Zimmermann*
> *from* Rejuvenating Impulses in Waldorf
> Education

Bibliography

1. Zimmermann, Heinz. ***Rejuvenating Impulses in Waldorf Education*** (original in German ***Von den Auftriebskraften in der Erziehung*** by Verlag am Goetheanum), Canada: Pegasus Publishing, 2003.

2. Zimmermann, Heinz. ***Speaking, Listening, Understanding: The Art of Creating Conscious Conversation,*** Hudson, NY: Lindisfarne Books, Steiner Books, 2004.

3. Mepham, Trevor, ed. ***Teachers Helping Teachers, Mentoring in Steiner Waldorf Schools,*** Forest Row, Sussex RH18 5JA, United Kingdom: Steiner/Waldorf Schools Fellowship, 2001. www.steinerwaldorf.org.uk

4. Flynn, Virginia and Ann Matthews, eds. ***"Elementary Education Project on Mentoring and Curriculum,"*** Pedagogical Consulting Colloquium, Fair Oaks, CA: AWSNA Publications, April 2002. www.awsna.org.

5. Avison, Kevin. ***A Handbook for Waldorf Class Teachers,*** Forest Row, Sussex RH18 5JA, United Kingdom: Steiner/Waldorf Schools Fellowship, 2001. www.steinerwaldorf.org.uk

6. Rawson, Martyn and Brien Masters. ***Towards Creative Teaching, Working with the Curriculum of Classes 1 to 8 in Steiner Waldorf Schools,*** Forest Row, Sussex RH18 5JA, United Kingdom: Steiner/Waldorf Schools Fellowship, 1997. www.steinerwaldorf.org.uk

7. Steiner, Rudolf. ***Awakening to Community,*** 10 lectures translated by Marjorie Spock. Spring Valley, NY: Anthroposophic Press, 1974.

Appendices

Appendix A
Criteria for Healthy Waldorf Classrooms

Appendix B
Seven Questions

Appendix C
Capacities, Skills and Support

Criteria for Healthy Waldorf Classrooms

Mentoring and Evaluation Criteria

The following aspects provide a basis for observation in grades one through eight. This list may be used either by a mentor (in a long-term confidential relationship to the teacher) or an evaluator, who will then provide a report of the visit.

Evaluators may need one hour or one week. Time should also be taken to observe the students during the recess time. Also, it may be recommended to come back once more during the term. Be sure that the report has the school, the date and the subject of the lesson. Ideally speaking, evaluators should review the contents of the report with the teacher visited before submitting it to the school.

Important Note: Useful as such a list may be, it may be the cause of one of the gravest mistakes we could make. This would be to draw any conclusions from these observations and perhaps miss the fact that this class and this teacher truly belong together and that the class is thriving, regardless of any number of "negative aspects" which we think could be significantly improved.

– Else Göttgens

Relationships

Is there warmth between the teacher and the children?

How do the children greet the teacher? Is there eye
contact, and is there a warm handshake?

How are the relationships between the children?

What is the spirit of the class? Is there enthusiasm and
receptivity?

Do the children listen well?

Do the children know their routine, their place?

Can the students work independently?

How are the work habits and problem-solving skills of
the children?

Are the students making an effort?

Are the children pale or rosy-cheeked?

Do the students behave with respect, with manners?

Is there an allowance for the spontaneous?

Wholeness of the Lesson

Does the teacher use appropriate images?

How does the teacher use the nights? What is the
nature of the review?

Is there a 50/50 balance between the initiative of the
teacher and that of the children?

How does the teacher incorporate or address the
temperaments of the students?

Is there laughter during the lesson?

Is there wholeness to the lesson, a balance of all
aspects?

Are there smooth transitions between activities?

Is there a concentrated bookwork time?

What is the quality of the books made by the
children?
What is the focus for the whole block?
What is the quality of the children's movements?
What is the quality of the children's speech?
Is there new material?
Is the on-going material still challenging?
Punctuality – does the lesson begin and end in a
timely way?
What is the end of the lesson like? Is there a moment
of "taking in"?
What is the demeanor of the children as they leave?

Professionalism
Are the methods appropriate to the developmental
stage of the children?
Are all of the children actively engaged in learning?
Are the individual differences of the children being
addressed?
Does the teacher keep a record of developing
capacities and skills?
Are there challenges to improve speech and grammar?
Is there mental math review?
What is the quality of the children's work?
Are the basic skills appropriate to the age level?
Is there an open-heartedness to imaginations?
How does the teacher handle discipline?
What is the children's response to correction?
Does the teacher teach the fundamentals – holding
the pencil, posture, seeing, etc.?

What is the predominant temperament of the teacher?

How does the teacher balance his or her own temperament?

Academic competence of the teacher? Competent presentations?

Can we observe anything in relation to the preparation of the teacher?

Does the teacher distract the students?

Use of the teacher's voice – pitch, variety of tone, loudness, etc.

Teacher's language skills – grammar, sentence structure, vocabulary, giving instructions, etc.

Is the teacher's handwriting clear?

Is the teacher's artistic skill adequate?

How does the teacher move about the classroom?

Is there appropriate attire, neatness and cleanliness?

Classroom Environment

Is there beauty in the classroom, appropriate pictures on the walls, etc.?

Is there tidiness and cleanliness?

Are the classroom and materials well organized?

Are the desks, chairs, tables of appropriate size for the children?

Is there attention to airflow, temperature and light?

If there are plants, are they well tended?

The list above was a result of the combined efforts of three groups of experienced teachers meeting in the AWSNA Mentor Collaboration Seminars during January, February and March of 2000.

AWSNA Pedagogical Advisors' Colloquium
Appendix B

Seven Questions

Out of her work in Waldorf schools, Else Göttgens has developed seven questions that she often gives to new teachers to ask themselves at the end of each day. After reviewing these points, the teacher can make plans for the next lesson on the next day.

1. Have I given them real and appropriate ***images or pictures*** in my story-telling or have I given them concepts/judgments?

2. Have I ***used the night?*** Has it come back differently from the children? Have I properly reviewed the lesson?

3. Has every child made at least some ***effort?***

4. Have I translated as much as possible from the main lesson into ***movement?***

5. Have I made the children laugh? Was there an ebb and flow, ***a real breathing,*** in the lesson?

6. Have I addressed one or more of the
   temperaments?

7. Have I taught ***something new*** – a new skill, some
   knowledge or a variation on an existing theme?

Capacities, Skills and Support

Capacities

Create the conditions to foster, nurture and develop the capacities of:

- Self-discipline
- Interest in learning
- Will to work
- Self-confidence
- Ability for independent thinking
- Gifts/challenges—self-knowledge
- Appreciation of others' gifts and challenges
- Literacy
- Numeracy
- Openness to the world and interest in the world
- Self-expression (clarity and articulation)
- Sense for living geography/history
- Creativity in the will/work and initiative
- Harmony of the physical body
- Appreciation for the uniqueness of the human being/ nature
- Phenomenology (keen sense of observation)
- Empathy/compassion
- Sense of wonder
- Imagination
- Analysis/synthesis
- Integrity
- Unlimited sense of others and self-potential
- Responsibility of self and world
- Humility
- Sense of humor

Skills

- Listening and note-taking
- Reading comprehension
- Creative/expressive writing
- Expository research
- Facility in math processes/calculation and application
- Spatial reasoning
- Objective observational skills
- Memory/recall, auditory and visual recall
- Problem-solving strategies
- Test-taking skills
- Research skills
- Social skills (collaboration, listening, impulse control)
- Competence in a second language
- Sight-reading music
- Physical skills
- Manual skills
- Artistic skills
- Public speaking
- Fundamentals of drama and stage awareness
- Speech and trained articulation
- Handwriting

Educational Support

- Thresholds met at appropriate levels
- Assessments for 2nd and 6th graders
- Outside experts to help with evaluating individual students
- Catalog of outside resources available within the community
- Training for teachers in assessing learning difficulties/disorders
- In-school tutoring for diagnosed needs
- Extra lesson teacher
- How to work with parents
- Good documentation and communication with parents
- Care groups

Notes